About Skill Builders Phonics

by Deborah Morris

Welcome to RBP Books' Skill Builders series. Like our Summer Bridge Activities collection, the Skill Builders series is designed to make learning both fun and rewarding.

The Skill Builders Phonics books are based on the premise that mastering language skills builds confidence and enhances a student's entire educational experience. A fundamental factor in learning to read is a strong phonics foundation, beginning with an awareness of the alphabet, understanding phonemic relationships and the concept of words, and moving onto word recognition.

Phonics Grade 2 contains pages on initial, ending, and medial consonants and moves on to vowels, compound words and syllabication, blends, digraphs, diphthongs, inflectional endings, and contractions, with review pages to reinforce important concepts.

A critical thinking section includes exercises to help develop higher-order thinking skills.

Learning is more effective when approached with an element of fun and enthusiasm—just as most children approach life. That's why the Skill Builders combine entertaining and academically sound exercises with eye-catching graphics and fun themes—to make reviewing basic skills at school or home fun and effective, for both you and your budding scholars.

Table of Contents

Initial Consonants

Say the name of the picture. Print the capital and small letters for the beginning sound.

Final Consonants

Say the name of the picture. Print the letter for the ending sound.

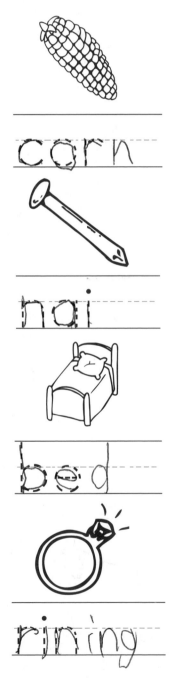

Medial Consonants

Say the name of each picture. Draw a line from the picture to the letter for the middle sound.

Example:

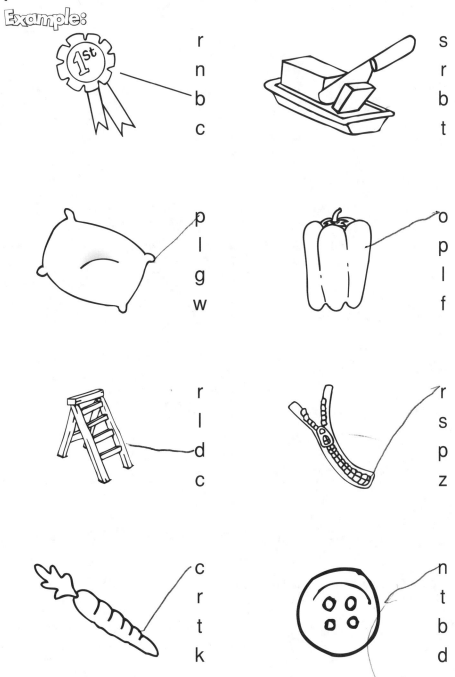

r
n
b
c

s
r
b
t

p
l
g
w

o
p
l
f

r
l
d
c

r
s
p
z

c
r
t
k

n
t
b
d

Phonics Grade 2—RBP0016

Short Vowels: *a*

Draw a line through the three rhyming words.
Lines can go across, down, or on a diagonal.

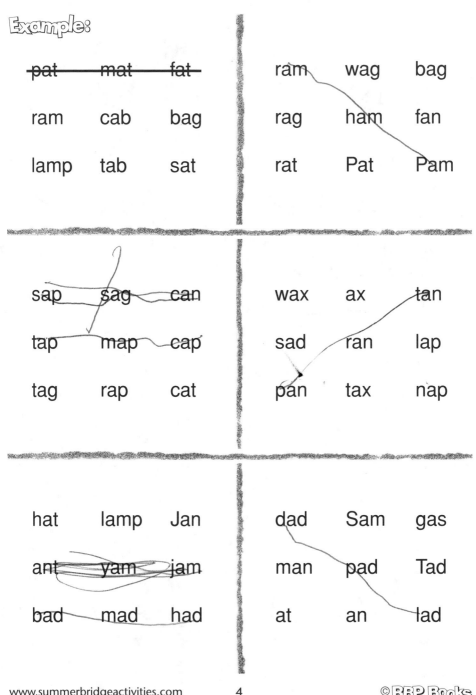

Example:

~~pat~~	~~mat~~	~~fat~~
ram	cab	bag
lamp	tab	sat

ram	wag	bag
rag	ham	fan
rat	Pat	Pam

sap	sag	can
tap	map	cap
tag	rap	cat

wax	ax	tan
sad	ran	lap
pan	tax	nap

hat	lamp	Jan
ant	yam	jam
bad	mad	had

dad	Sam	gas
man	pad	Tad
at	an	lad

Short Vowels: *i*

Choose a word to complete each sentence.
Put an X on the word. Print it in the space.

1. Mom let us fish in the _Pond_ .

bib
rip
sink

2. So Kim put in six _____ .

hit
pig
fish

3. Look! They like to _____ .

rip
fit
swim

4. I _____ I was a fish.

wish
wink
will

5. Will they _____ in the tank?

ring
fit
tip

6. We fill up the _____ and give them a trip.

fig
dish
lick

7. The big tank is a _____ .

dig
mix
hit

Short Vowels: *o*

Circle the best answer. Underline the short o sounds.

Example:

1. You can pet a <u>hot</u> <u>dog</u>.　　　　　**yes (no)**

2. A frog lives in a pond.　　　　　**yes no**

3. Mom can sit on a log.　　　　　**yes no**

4. The rock on the sun is hot.　　　　　**yes no**

5. Put the fox in the pot.　　　　　**yes no**

6. Tom has a lot of socks.　　　　　**yes no**

7. You can lock the box.　　　　　**yes no**

8. A doll likes to mop.　　　　　**yes no**

Short Vowels: *e*

Help Denise get Pepper to the vet. Print the picture name next to the picture.

Word Bank
jet
bed
vet
web
nest
tent

Short Vowels: *u*

Choose one word for each sentence to make a silly story. Circle the word. Then print it on the space.

1. Today I rode on a _____.

sub
cub
skunk

2. Then I took a nap in the _____.

tub
jug
mud

3. For lunch I ate _____.

bugs
gum
nuts

4. A _____ ran off with my mug.

bus
slug
duck

5. So I sat in a _____ in the sun.

rug
bun
cup

Long Vowels: *a*

If a word has two vowels, the first vowel says its alphabet name. That is the long sound. The second vowel is silent.

Example: cave, date, rain

Print the name of each picture below. Then circle the name in the puzzle.

cake   smile   rain

plate   sat bucket rack

e k a r f r p w
p c p s a t a k
z l l f c e i a
c a a s e k l i
k g r t w a x g
c w r a e c i u
a a m t i n l u
m y l b f n v v

Long Vowels: *i*

Ty and Mike are going to do something. Choose a word from the backpack that rhymes. Print it on the line.

Backpack
side
mile
fly
line
~~bike~~

Example:

1. Get the one I like, the big red bike.

2. Hurry, Ty, we have to _____.

3. I have mine, so get in _____.

4. Now, when we ride, stay on my _____.

5. It takes a while to go a _____.

What are Ty and Mike going to do? Use some of these long *i* words to write a sentence telling what you think they are doing.

bike pine hike ride mile time line side mine

_____

_____

_____

_____

Long Vowels: *o*

Circle the word that answers the riddle. Then print it on the line.

Example:

1. A car can ride on it. _road_

hope
(road)
rope

2. We wash our hands with it. _____

toe
rose
soap

3. It is green and likes to hop. _____

boat
toad
goat

4. We put it on when it is cold. _____

moat
coat
nose

5. I write it to tell something. _____

note
bone
soak

6. A dog likes to bite on it. _____

bone
coat
soap

Long Vowels: e

Find the long e words in the puzzle. Circle them. Use them in the story below.

f	e	e	t	q	m	y	e
d	m	j	e	e	p	j	t
g	z	m	k	i	f	u	d
o	k	z	k	a	e	b	w
q	e	e	r	t	b	b	w
u	c	e	a	s	t	t	i
k	e	e	w	i	c	w	a
d	s	t	o	n	h	s	l

Word Bank
sea
feet
beak
week
east
jeep
tree

Example:

I had a dream last WEEK. I saw a seal by the

_____. It had a _____ for a nose and

six _____. It was in a _____ with a

red seat. The seal went _____ to see a leaf

on a _____.

Long Vowels: *u*

Look at the Word Bank. Choose two words that tell about each picture. Then write the words on the lines provided.

| **Word Bank** |
| cute musical tube flute tune bugle Sue used |

1.

2.

3.

4.

Compound Words

A compound word is two words put together to make one. Help Robin Hood shoot an arrow from one word to another to make a compound word.

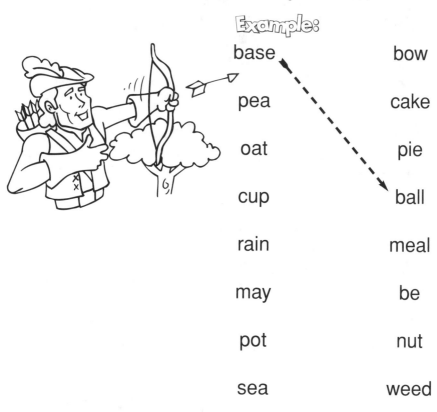

Example:

base	bow
pea	cake
oat	pie
cup	ball
rain	meal
may	be
pot	nut
sea	weed

Print the compound words.

1. _____

2. _____

3. _____

4. _____

5. _____

6. _____

7. _____

8. _____

Compound Crossword

Print the word under the clue. Then fill in the boxes in the crossword puzzle.

Across	**Down**
2. A hill for ants.	**1.** A pack for your back.
3. Corn you can pop.	**4.** A coat for the rain.
6. A cake cooked on a pan.	**5.** A boat that you sail.
7. A box to hold mail.	
8. A box full of sand.	

Two-Syllable Words

Words have parts called syllables. Each syllable has one vowel sound.

Example: cat = one syllable

but·ton = two syllables

The words with two syllables are underlined. Circle each vowel you hear in the underlined words.

1. They have <u>open</u> <u>boxes</u> <u>inside</u> the shop

2. <u>Megan</u> puts a <u>pillow</u> in the <u>basket</u>.

3. My <u>kitten</u> has a <u>yellow</u> <u>ribbon</u> on its neck.

4. I have a <u>ticket</u> in my <u>pocket</u> for the pet show.

5. My <u>kitten's</u> name is <u>Rabbit</u>.

6. He wins <u>second</u> place—<u>hurray</u>!

Two-Syllable Words

Circle the vowels you hear in the words in the boxes.
Write the two-syllable word on the line below.

kite	got
bed	open

1. _____

tree	boxes
cake	sea

2. _____

dime	note
inside	toad

3. _____

sand	mail
take	puppet

4. _____

mitten	best
tent	socks

5. _____

egg	feet
road	wagons

6. _____

Print the two-syllable word by the same number on
the line to make a sentence.

(1)_____ the (2)_____ and

(3)_____ you'll find a (4)_____,

a (5)_____, and (6)_____.

Words Ending in *-le*

Choose words from the Word Bank to solve the riddles below. Print the answers on the lines.

Word Bank

whistle puddle giggle ~~candles~~ apple bubbles

Example:

1. You put them on your birthday cake.

candles

2. This makes a sound when you blow it.

_____

3. You get wet when you jump in this.

_____

4. You do this when someone tickles you.

_____

5. This fruit makes a tasty snack.

_____

6. You can blow these with gum.

_____

Words Ending in *-le*

In the space below, print the number of the sentence that tells about the picture.

1. Look, Mom, those people are on the table.

2. How did that turtle get in the bottle?

3. That apple will fall on the candle.

4. Do all eagles blow bubbles?

Hard and Soft c

When **c** is followed by **e, i,** or **y**, it often has a soft sound. It sounds like /s/.

Example: face

Choose a word from the Word Bank to print on the line. Color the **hard c** words red. Color the **soft c** words yellow.

Word Bank			
fence	nice	race	rice

_____

Two little mice who are twice as _____,

took a cab into space to _____.

"Come down here," said Cyndi,

"This place is too windy."

Can't you sit on the _____

and eat _____?

Hard and Soft c

Court   **Cecil**

| price |
| lace |
| carrot |
| cereal |
| cones |
| cane |
| pencil |
| clock |
| ice |
| face |
| celery |
| case |

Court and Cecil are fishing in the sea. Print the
hard c words on the lines under **Court**. Print the
soft c words under **Cecil**.

                                       Phonics Grade 2—RBP0016

Hard and Soft *g*

Fill in the circle indicating whether the g is hard or soft.

Example:

1. gate ● hard ○ soft

2. gym ○ hard ○ soft

3. gem ○ hard ○ soft

4. large ○ hard ○ soft

5. gift ○ hard ○ soft

6. stage ○ hard ○ soft

7. dragon ○ hard ○ soft

8. goat ○ hard ○ soft

9. page ○ hard ○ soft

10. giraffe ○ hard ○ soft

11. huge ○ hard ○ soft

12. cage ○ hard ○ soft

Hard and Soft *g*

Color the boxes with **soft g** words orange. Color the boxes with **hard g** words green. What do you see?

giraffe	page	gem	huge	gate
gym	goat	egg	game	dragon
giant	good	gold	dog	wag
age	gaze	stage	George	got
large	gum	gap	wage	tag
cage	magic	gentle	dodge	bag

Review

To review compound words, syllables, words ending in -**le**, and **hard** and **soft c** and **g** words, read the story. Print the answers on the lines.

Johnny Appleseed

Johnny put on his backpack. Then he went out the gate of his backyard. Inside his pack was a large cup of apple seeds. He gave some to nice people. They gave him eggs and oatmeal to eat in return. The planted seeds were like magic. The next day the little trees were huge. There were apples on all the tables.

1. Johnny put on a _____.

2. People were _____ and gave him _____ and _____ to eat.

3. The seeds were like _____.

4. _____ trees looked _____.

5. Apples were on all the _____.

Blends: *r*

A consonant blend is two or more consonants together. The sounds blend, but you can hear each one.

Example: <u>gr</u>ape, <u>br</u>ake, <u>tr</u>ee

Circle the picture name.

dress   drag   drink | brake   bring   branch | grade   grass   grape

from   fruit   frost | trail   trade   truck | drum   drive   drip

price   press   prince | free   frost   frog | trike   trim   tree

Phonics Grade 2—RBP0016

Blends: *l*

Say each word. Listen to the blend. Print the word where it belongs.

Example:	Word Bank		
clock	glitter	globe	plane
flap	slipper	class	block
plant	clue	play	flag
blade	blow	flame	slow
flake	closet	glue	plum
slide	glass	blue	slick

glad	**flat**	**close**
		~~clock~~

plate	**black**	**slip**

Blends: *s*

Draw a squiggly line from each picture to its beginning blend.

Example:

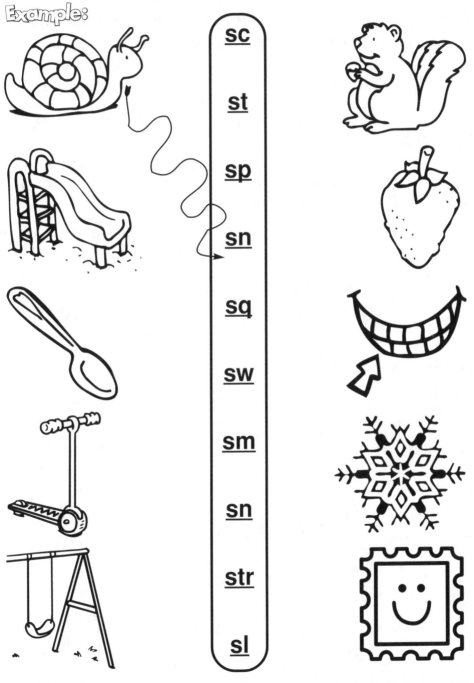

sc

st

sp

sn

sq

sw

sm

sn

str

sl

Final Blends

Remember, a consonant blend is two or more consonants together. The sounds blend, but you can hear each one. Read the list of words and notice the consonant blends at the end of the words. Choose the correct word to complete each sentence and write it in the blank.

1. We like to _____ in the woods.

clamp
camp

2. But some land has tree _____.

stamps
stumps

3. It is my task to set up the _____.

tent
rent

4. We hang our milk from the tree _____.

bunk
trunk

5. I need a hand to take the _____ on the river.

raft
left

y as a Vowel

Sometimes the consonant **y** sounds like the long-vowel sound of **e** or **i**.

Example: puppy

Circle the word with the same **y** sound as the picture.

dry ~~body~~ why

50

happy very shy

daddy spy (Ty)

sandy try sleepy

my try tiny

sly funny by

jolly fry dry

fly silly rocky

try spy windy

y as a Vowel

When **y** is at the end of a one-syllable word, it usually sounds like a **long i**.

Example: sky

In the Word Bank, circle the **y** words with the **long i** sound. Then find each word in the word search.

```
g  y  k  y  g  i  b  w  m  i
w  r  j  l  j  c  y  u  y  j
h  f  s  f  t  p  d  h  k  v
y  a  l  k  s  d  s  j  c  y
r  o  c  k  y  y  a  i  u  n
o  z  m  p  r  v  y  y  l  a
s  m  y  r  y  l  l  n  u  m
i  r  u  q  r  o  i  n  h  m
d  h  b  p  c  m  l  u  j  y
p  t  r  y  d  d  s  b  e  l
```

Review: Blends and *y* as a Vowel

Put the number of each word below on the line that helps finish the story.

<u>**Word Bank**</u>

1. raft	4. trunk	7. spoon
2. lucky	5. sneaky	8. try
3. scream	6. dress	9. stuck

1. "Let's play _____ up," said Blake.

2. Mandy got the dusty _____ from inside the closet.

3. " _____ to lift the lid with your hands."

4. "It's _____ !" Blake said with an angry cry.

5. Suddenly, Ty jumped out with a _____ .

6. "That was a very _____ trick," Mandy said with a smile.

Do you think Mandy was mad at Ty?

Consonant Digraphs: *ch*, *sh*, *th*, and *wh*

A consonant digraph is two consonants that make one sound.

    Example: chip, shut, then, why

Say each word from the Word Bank. Print it on the line under the picture with the same digraph as the word.

Example:	Word Bank		
chimp	thin	teeth	why
shut	white	shake	cherry
that	each	when	shoe
wish	wheel	this	beach

chimp

Consonant Digraphs: *ch, sh, th,* and *wh*

Circle the best word. Print it on the line.

1. Sometimes I like to _____.

shop
shell
shape

2. This _____ is very nice to sit on.

chip
such
chair

3. I'm hungry. I wish it was time for

_____
_____.

much
cheese
lunch

4. Sherry will _____ a nice white shirt for Dad.

check
choose
bunch

5. She sees _____ I love to eat with milk.

which
what
when

6. I reach for the fresh _____.

chip
peach
change

Consonant Digraphs: *kn*

The consonant digraph **kn** sounds like /n/.
Print a **kn** word from the Word Bank that rhymes
with each word listed below.

Word Bank				
knot	knife	knight	knee	knew
knob	knock	kneel	know	knit

1. feel _____

2. blow _____

3. clock _____

4. rob _____

5. free _____

6. mitt _____

7. life _____

8. stew _____

Consonant Digraphs: *wr*

The consonant digraph **wr** sounds like /r/.
Here are some digraph riddles. Choose the best answer
from the Word Bank. Print the word on the line.

Word Bank					
wrong	wren	write	wreck	wrench	wrap
wrist	wrestle	wreath	wrinkles	wriggle	wring

1. People sometimes hang me on the wall.

2. When you get a gift you rip me off the outside.

3. Mom irons me out of her dresses.

4. A lot of dads have me as a helpful tool.

5. People put a watch on me.

6. I am a tiny bird that eats worms.

Digraph Review

Say each word in the row. Listen for its digraph sound. Draw an X on the one that does not have the same sound.

1. wash   sheep   shoe   this

2. white   with   when   what

3. chick   cash   change   cheese

4. knee   which   knob   knock

5. this   with   thing   dish

6. shut   shake   why   wish

7. wrong   know   write   wrist

8. teeth   chimp   each   cherry

Digraph Review Crossword

Read the clue; then look for the word in the Word Bank. Print the answer in the puzzle.

Word Bank			
knee	sheep	knock	thing
wrong	write	beach	teeth
cheese	bench	shells	dish

Across

3. There is one of these in the middle of your leg.

5. A mouse loves to eat this.

6. You brush these after eating.

Down

1. Kids do this with a pencil on paper.

2. This has lots of sand and shells.

4. I find these on the beach.

ar Words

When **r** follows a vowel, it makes the vowel sound different. The **ar** says the name of the letter **r**. Print each word under the jar that holds a word it rhymes with.

Word Bank					
smart	lark	dark	dart	card	park
part	yard	mark	tart	lard	shard

hard   **cart**   **shark**

or Words

When **r** follows a vowel, it makes the vowel sound different.

Example: for, tore

Circle the word in each box that does not rhyme.
Print the word on the line below the box.

porch	(tore)
torch	scorch

1. tore

horn	popcorn
horse	torn

2. _____

fort	porch
short	sport

3. _____

born	storm
thorn	corn

4. _____

pork	stork
cork	shore

5. _____

short	more
store	fore

6. _____

Write a sentence using some of the words.

_____

_____

_____

ir, *er*, and *ur* Words

When **r** follows a vowel, it makes the vowel sound different.
   Example: first, her, purse
Say each word. Look for the vowel followed by an **r**.
Draw a line from the word to the matching **vowel + r**.

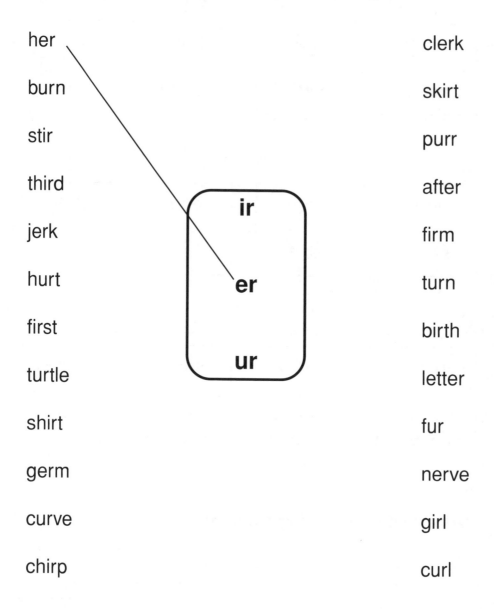

her   clerk

burn   skirt

stir   purr

third   after

              ir

jerk   firm

hurt   **er**   turn

first   birth

              ur

turtle   letter

shirt   fur

germ   nerve

curve   girl

chirp   curl

Review Words: *ar, ir, er, ur,* and *or*

Read this silly story and notice the underlined words. Then read the list of words below and find one that rhymes with each word in the story. Write the number of the rhyming word in the blank.

I was sitting on the (1) <u>torch</u> the other night. It was very, very (2) <u>park</u> and (3) <u>formy</u>. Suddenly, a (4) <u>fork</u> came flying into the (5) <u>card</u>. "Help!" it said. "A (6) <u>curl</u> is after me."

"Go to the (7) <u>more,</u>" I said. "There is a (8) <u>force</u> waiting to take you (9) <u>car</u> away. Don't (10) <u>furry</u>, it will not (11) <u>dirt</u> you." Afterwards, I (12) <u>burned</u> (13) <u>forks</u> are not very (14) <u>dart</u>!

___horse   ___smart   ___storks   ___shore   ___ girl

___porch   ___hurt   ___ far   ___ yard   ___ stork

___dark   ___stormy   ___worry   ___learned

Contractions: *will*

A contraction is a way to make two words into one.
To make the new word, we leave some letters out. An
apostrophe (') is used to show that letters are missing.
Some contractions are made with the word **will**.

Do contraction subtraction: I + will – wi = I'll

Choose a word from the Word Bank below that can
take the place of the two words. Print it on the line.

Word Bank		
I'll	you'll	we'll
they'll	she'll	he'll

1. you will _____

2. we will _____

3. he will _____

4. they will_____

5. I will _____

6. she will_____

Contractions: *not*

Some contractions are made with **not**.

Do contraction subtraction: is + not – o = isn't
Underline two words in each sentence that could
make one of the contractions in the Word Bank. Print
the contraction on the line.

Word Bank				
isn't	weren't	doesn't	haven't	didn't
can't	don't	couldn't	hasn't	aren't

1. Justin is sick and has
not come to the park.

2. He did not get chicken
pox when I did.

3. Now Justin has red
dots, and I do not.

4. Jeremy, Kirk, and Ty
have not gone to visit.

5. But that is not going to
stop me.

Why aren't Jeremy, Kirk, and Ty going to visit?

Contractions: *is*

Some contractions are made with the word is.
    Do contraction subtraction: it + is − i = it's
Print the contraction from each sentence by its number.
Next, print the two words that make up the contraction.

1. "How's your tarantula?" I asked Whitney.

2. "I think she's lost somewhere under my bed."

3. "That's too bad," I said, as I turned to run.

4. "Hey, what's your hurry, Marci?"

5. "It's just a joke. She is in her cage."

1. _____ = _____

2. _____ = _____

3. _____ = _____

4. _____ = _____

5. _____ = _____

Contractions: *have*

Some contractions are made with the word **have**.
When making a contraction with **have**, contraction
subtraction takes away two letters.

   Do contraction subtraction: I + have – ha = I've
Do contraction subtraction with the underlined
words. Follow the example.

Example:

1. "Corinne, <u>I have</u> taken a picture of the mom and her baby."

$$ I + have - ha = I've $$

2. "<u>You have</u> worked hard today."

_____ + _____ – ha = _____

3. "<u>We have</u> seen plenty of deer before."

_____ + _____ – ha = _____

4. "<u>They have</u> gone back into the forest."

_____ + _____ – ha = _____

Contractions: *am*, *are*, and *us*

Some contractions are made with the words **am**, **are**, or **us**.
  Do contraction subtraction: I + am − a = I'm
                                we + are − a = we're
                                let + us − u = let's
Read each sentence. Find the contraction. Put the number of the sentence next to the two words in the Word Bank that make the contraction.

<u>Word Bank</u>

____ let us   ____ you are   ____ I am

____ they are   ____ we are

1. "Let's go swimming in the lake," Peter yelled.

2. "We're going to take Abbey, too," Porter added.

3. "You're sure they let dogs on the beach?" Mom asked.

4. "I'm sure," said Emerson as they all ran to swim.

5. "They're always running all over and barking."

Contraction Review

In each line of the poem are words than can be made into a contraction. Put an X on the words and print the contraction on the line.

1. I am doing contraction subtraction, _____

_____

2. You are going to get to play too. _____

_____

3. I will take away one or two letters, _____

_____

4. They will never be missed, it is true. _____

_____

5. The apostrophe is not forgotten, _____

_____

6. Some things are not ever left out. _____

_____

7. Since you have seen it before, _____

_____

8. Let us try it once more, _____

_____

9. And when we are done we will shout. _____

_____   _____

Vowel Pairs: *ai* and *ay*

When two vowels are together, the first says its alpha-bet name (long vowel sound), and the second one is quiet. The vowel pairs **ai** and **ay** say the **long a** sound.
Example: pail, day
Circle the correct word that completes each sentence.

1. I like to see the (nail, snail, pain) move slowly on the wet grass.

2. It leaves a slimy (mail, wait, trail).

3. The brown shell on its back is very (pay, may, plain).

4. It may take all (clay, tray, day) for it to cross the yard.

5. But I can't (stay, pay, way) here and play.

6. Dad and I are going to (sail, paint, ray) the house.

7. We have a (pail, maid, stain) of gray paint.

8. I hope we're done before it starts to (chain, say, rain).

Vowel Pairs: *ee* and *ea*

Holdon June 30th 2011

The vowel pairs **ee** and **ea** say the **long e sound**.

Example: feet, peach

Color in the circle of the correct word that completes the sentence.

1. Yesterday we went to the shore to swim in the ___wat___ .

- ○ tree
- ○ peep
- ● sea

---

2. It seemed too cold, but the _____ loved it.

- ○ jeans
- ○ beans
- ● seals

---

3. Seals don't have _____. They have flippers.

- ● feet
- ○ deep
- ○ each

---

4. For their morning _____, they eat fish and shellfish.

- ○ seed
- ● meal
- ○ jeep

---

5. It would be _____ to be a seal.

- ● easy
- ○ seen
- ○ three

---

6. They just bask in the sun on the _____.

- ○ peach
- ○ peal
- ● beach

Vowel Pairs: *oe, oa,* and *ow*

The vowel pairs **oe, oa,** and sometimes **ow** say the **long o** sound. Put an X on the word from the Word Bank to complete each riddle. Write the word on the line.

Word Bank			
toe	Joe	goat	rainbow
float	bow	coat	loaf
bowl	doe	mow	soap

1. There are five of me on each foot.
Do you know what I am? _____

2. You use me to wash your hands.
Do you know what I am? _____

3. You put me on in the winter.
Do you know what I am? _____

4. I come out after it rains.
Do you know what I am? _____

5. My baby is called a fawn.
Do you know what I am? _____

6. You put cereal in me.
Do you know what I am? _____

Vowel Pairs Review

Word Search
Find these vowel-pair words in the word search below.

Word Bank			
nail	soak	beet	blow
toe	seem	clay	know
peach	wait	coach	seal

```
w h w a i t d w z o
w s r q w o n k v w
g e r h e h g a y v
w e t z c b c a s b
l m o e g a l a l m
p o b s e c e o o t
l w s v e b w p x c
i r c o i a v k u e
a h c z a m l x o n
n a z t i k x t b l
```

Vowel Digraphs: *oo*

A vowel digraph is two vowels together that make either a long sound, a short sound, or a new sound.
    Example: look, zoo
Say each word in the Word Bank. Print the word under the picture that makes the same sound.

Word Bank

cook	good	boot	food	hook	took
room	broom	foot	wood	shook	brook
tooth	zoo	too	spoon	look	soon	noon

1. _____
2. _____
3. _____
4. _____
5. _____
6. _____
7. _____
8. _____
9. _____
10. _____

1. _____
2. _____
3. _____
4. _____
5. _____
6. _____
7. _____
8. _____
9. _____

Vowel Digraphs: *ea*

The vowel digraph **ea** makes the **short e** sound.
　　Example: sweat
Choose a word from the Word Bank to complete each
sentence. Put one letter on each line.

Word Bank			
bread	ready	weather	breakfast
spread	thread	breath	meadow
feather	heavy	head	deaf

1. To make toast we use wheat __ __ __ ☑ __.

2. I ☐ __ __ __ __ __ grape jelly on with a knife.

3. In cold ☐ __ __ __ __ __ __ we have hot chocolate.

4. Mom has it __ ☐ __ __ __ early in the morning.

5. Steve puts on his __ __ ☐ __ __ coat to go outside.

6. Carrie has a coat that's light as a __ __ __ ☐ __ __ __.

7. Alex has a hat on his __ ☐ __ __.

8. I can see my __ ☐ __ __ __ __ fog on the car window.

Use the letters in the boxes to answer the question,
What do you wear when it's cold?

__ __ ___ __ __ __ __ __

Vowel Digraphs: *au* and *aw*

The vowel digraphs **au** and **aw** both make the same sound. It is a tired sound—like when you yawn.

> **Example:** auto, yawn

Circle the word that names the picture.

straw   pause   saw

fault   raw   yawn

haul   auto   paw

autumn   laundry   crawl

hawk   because   dawn

applesauce   claw   fawn

Vowel Digraph Review

Say each picture name. Circle the digraph that makes the vowel sound in each name.

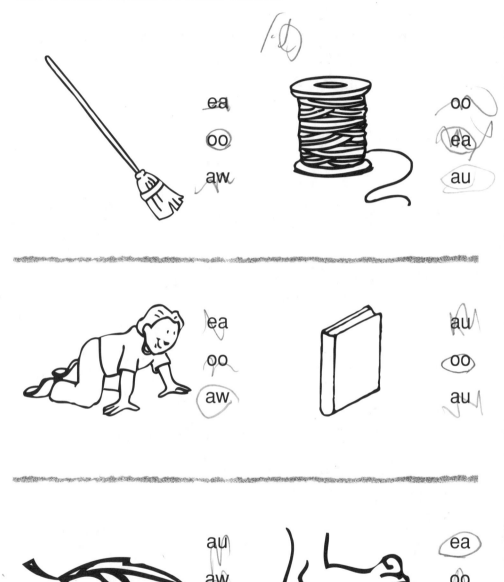

Diphthongs: *ou* and *ow*

Two letters blended together to create one sound make a diphthong.

Example: cloud, crown

Read each sentence. Circle all the **ou** and **ow** diphthongs in each sentence. Then print the word in the correct column on the next page.

1. We found our cat Scout just outside of town.

2. I don't know how, but maybe it was his loud meow.

3. Now he likes to hide behind the couch at our house.

4. Scout has a stuffed brown mouse.

5. Without a sound he holds it in his mouth.

Diphthongs: *ou* and *ow*

<u>**ou**</u>   <u>**ow**</u>

Diphthongs: *oi* and *oy*

Diphthongs **oi** and **oy** make the same sound.
Example: toy, foil
Say the picture name. Find the name in the Word
Bank. Print its number under the picture.

Word Bank			
1. spoil	2. noise	3. soil	4. toys
5. voice	6. boil	7. coins	8. foil
9. boy	10. oil	11. choice	12. point

Diphthongs: *ew*

Diphthong **ew** makes the **long u** sound.

Example: few

Put the number of the word next to the riddle that it answers.

Word Bank				
1. dew	2. flew	3. new	4. mew	5. Drew
6. stew	7. screw	8. crew	9. blew	10. chew

___ Who knew that this helps hold two boards together?

___ Who knew that a kitten makes this sound?

___ Who knew that this is a thick soup with carrots and beef?

___ Who knew that when you eat you do this with your teeth?

___ Who knew that this is water on grass in the morning?

___ Who knew that this is the opposite of *old*?

Diphthong Review: *ou, ow, oi, oy,* and *ew*

Use the diphthongs in the Sound Bank to complete the word below each picture.

Sound Bank				
ou	oy	ow	oi	ew

cr __ __ n

c __ __ l

n __ __ spaper

t __ __

cl __ __ d

sh __ __ er

n __ __

b __ __

n __ __ se

Inflectional Endings: -ed

A base word is a word to which an ending can be added.
   Example: rain + ed = rained
Add -ed to the base word (the words below each sentence). Print the word on the line.

1. Larry _____ to go see the parade.
      want

2. We _____ as the clowns _____ by.
      laugh   **pass**

3. They _____ and _____ at each other.
       jump   **yell**

4. Then, the band _____ as they _____.
                        play   **march**

5. We _____ when Kent _____ his tuba to wave.
      cheer   **raise**

6. The parade _____ just as it _____.
                  end   **rain**

Inflectional Endings: *-ing*

A base word is a word to which an ending can be added.
Example: sing + ing = singing
Print the letter of the word with the **-ing** ending that matches the base word.

_____ ask   **a.** kicking

_f_ sleep   **b.** munching

_____ munch   **c.** pushing

ing kick   **d.** jumping

_____ push   **e.** asking

_____ jump   **f.** sleeping

Finish adding an **-ing** ending to the base words below. Print the word on the line.

1. find + ing = _____

2. want + ing = _____

3. cheer + ing = _____

4. crack + ing = _____

5. stick + ing = _____

Inflectional Ending Review

1. Lee and Gene are _____ cars to get some money. **wash**

-ed
-ing

2. First they _____ a bucket with soapy water. **fill**

-ed
-ing

3. Next they are _____ with wet, sudsy rags. **clean**

-ed
-ing

4. Watch out! Someone is _____ with the hoses. **spray**

-ed
-ing

5. They _____ me, but Lee and Gene are getting very wet. **miss**

-ed
-ing

6. Oh, well! _____ hard can be fun too. **work**

-ed
-ing

Lunchroom Limerick

A limerick is a silly poem. It has five lines. Lines one, two, and five rhyme. Lines three and four rhyme. The limerick below has different endings for each line. You get to choose. Circle one ending for each line. Print your limerick on a piece of paper. You can mix and match to make many different limericks.

There was a young girl   in fifth grade,
Adelaide,
from Kinkade,

Whose   lunchtime kept getting delayed.
picnic was already made.
mom had made pink lemonade.

When she got   hungry enough,
meat that was tough,
done, it was rough,

There was   no more stuff,
just one cheese puff,
food on her cuff,

And her   sack lunch she wanted to trade.
class had to march in parade.
lunch was lost in the shade.

Brain Teaser

Read the riddle. Write what you think it is about.

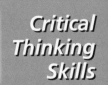
 Spy

I am sailing in a ship
Upon the deep blue sea.
 spy this down below.
It is big as a bus, looking at us
And spouting water at me.

What is it? _____

My grandmother has a locket.
It has no locks I see.
She keeps it in her pocket,
And away from me.
Sometimes she takes it out
And puts it on a shelf.
 spy it and I open it. All by myself!

Write a sentence telling what you think
is in the locket.

_____

I have lost them you see,
But they are not lost to me.
They are under my head on the bed.
If I lift up my pillow
 spy them and uh-oh!
In their spot I find a dollar instead.

What are they? _____

Choose Your Own Story

Choose a compound word from the next page that sounds right to complete each sentence. When you are done, you will have your own funny story. You may add -s to a word to help it sound right. You can make more than one story. Just use different words each time.

One day my friends and I were playing

_____. Suddenly I heard _____ shout.

There was a _____ waiting _____. The

people were wearing _____ and _____.

We wanted to see their _____, but it was

_____. So we ate _____ and

_____. Then we took a _____ home.

Draw a picture that goes with your story.

Compound Words

lunchtime	someone	horseshoe
streetcar	driveway	rowboat
spaceship	beehive	raincoat
applesauce	basketball	bathroom
pineapple	horsefly	somebody
dinnertime	butterfly	baseball
pancake	everyone	doughnut
swimsuit	sunflower	football
toolbox	toothpaste	peanut
everybody	seaweed	bathrobe
cupcake	popcorn	inside
outside	downtown	overall
overcoat	bedspread	beehive

Marshall's Pet

Circle all the words with **ar, ir, or, er,** and **ur** in the story about Marshall's pet on the next page. Remember, in these words, a vowel is followed by the **r**. Say each word. Listen to the sound. Print each word in the column below with the same sound.

ar	**or**	**er, ir, ur**

Marshall's Pet

Marshall wanted a pet. He had never had one before. His mom said to study hard to find the perfect one for him. He started with a visit to the pet store.

First he saw the puppy. Dogs are smart and fun to play with. But you have to work really hard. They need to learn lots of rules. Sometimes they dig in the dirt and need a bath. They bark at birds in the yard.

He saw the turtle next. Turtles need water for swimming. They curl up in their shells a lot. You never have to take one for a walk. A turtle doesn't take very much of your time.

Later, Marshall saw the kitten. He liked to pet its fur and feel it purr in his arms. Of course, cats don't do tricks very well.

Marshall started for home. He had a hard decision to make.

What pet do you think Marshall will get? Why?

Bats

You can find bats everywhere, but they prefer warm weather. Most bats don't like flying very far. They have wings, but they are not birds. Bats don't have feathers—they have fur.

Some people think bats are blind, but they aren't. They have very good eyesight. Bats can see better in the dark. They use their eyes, ears, and nose to find food.

Fruit-eating bats help spread seeds in the forest. Many bats help humans by eating insects. One brown bat can catch 600 mosquitoes in one hour! When a bat flies home, it usually likes to go to a cave. Some also like living under bridges and in mines. You can make a bat house from wood. Go to the library to find out how.

Bats

1. Where can you find bats?

_____evry wher_____

2. Bats don't have _feathers_ They have _fur_ .

3. They use their _____, _____, and _____ to find food.

4. What do some bats eat? _____

5. How many mosquitoes can one brown bat catch in an hour? _____

6. Where do bats live? _____

_____

Where in the World Is... ?

Find each word below in the word search. Then circle the word. Put a line through the ones you find.

Word Bank

yawn	dragon	sky	found
wagon	cereal	yard	choice
music	giraffe	nerve	screw
pillow	bride	chain	raining
whistle	clock	peach	space
carrots	prince	rainbow	strawberry
glitter	trunk	broom	laughed
rocky	thorn	feather	laundry

```
x  s  g  i  r  a  f  f  e  c  h  a  i  n  v
j  p  p  w  d  n  w  a  y  c  l  o  c  k  d
r  a  r  a  n  r  d  c  a  r  r  o  t  s  r
s  c  i  g  u  w  e  r  m  m  d  o  h  k  a
t  e  n  o  o  z  h  h  a  h  o  n  o  s  g
r  d  c  n  f  b  k  i  t  y  c  o  u  w  o
a  e  e  d  i  r  b  h  s  a  y  a  r  a  n
w  h  g  f  s  c  r  e  w  t  e  k  e  b  l
b  g  g  r  e  t  t  i  l  g  l  f  c  p  g
e  u  c  n  n  r  o  h  t  a  v  e  i  o  q
r  a  h  z  w  o  b  n  i  a  r  y  y  i  r
r  l  o  x  g  e  f  e  v  r  e  n  s  k  y
y  u  i  y  b  m  g  n  i  n  i  a  r  r  l
w  k  c  w  o  l  l  i  p  n  m  u  s  i  c
n  c  e  r  e  a  l  w  b  t  r  u  n  k  x
```

Answer Pages

Page 1

D, d	H, h	G, g	T, t
F, f	C, c	B, b	W, w

Page 2

n	p	l	b
d	k	g	w

Page 3

b	t	l	p
d	p	r	t

Page 4

pat, mat, fat	ram, ham, Pam
tap, map, cap	pan, ran, tan
bad, mad, had	dad, pad, lad

Page 5

1. sink   **2.** fish   **3.** swim   **4.** wish
5. fit   **6.** dish   **7.** hit

Page 6 (*Yes* or *no* may vary.)

1. no, hot dog   **2.** yes, frog, pond
3. yes, Mom, log   **4.** yes, on, rock, hot
5. no, fox, pot   **6.** yes, Tom, lot, socks
7. yes, lock, box   **8.** no, doll, mop

Page 7

nest	jet	bed
tent	web	vet

Page 8

Answers will vary.

Page 9

cake	face	rain
plate	pail	rake

```
e k a r  f  r  p  w
p  c p s  a  t  a  k
z  l  l  f  c  e  i  a
c  a  a  s  e  k  l  i
k  g  r  t  w  a  x  g
c  w  r  a  e  c  i  u
a  a  m  t  i  n  l  u
m  y  l  b  f  n  v  v
```

Page 10

1. bike   **2.** fly   **3.** line
4. side   **5.** mile
Answers will vary.

Page 11

1. road   **2.** soap   **3.** toad
4. coat   **5.** note   **6.** bone

Page 12

```
f e e t  q m y  e
d m  j e e p  j  t
g z m k  i  f  u  d
o k z  k a e b  w
q  e e r t  b b  w
u c  e a s  t  t  i
k e e w  i  c w  a
d s  t  o n h s  l
```

week, sea, beak, feet, jeep, east, tree

Page 13

Answers may vary.
1. cute, Sue   **2.** musical, tune, bugle
3. musical, tune, flute   **4.** used, tube

Page 14

baseball	peanut	oatmeal	cupcake
rainbow	maybe	potpie	seaweed

Page 15

Across	Down
2. anthill	**1.** backpack
3. popcorn	**4.** raincoat
6. pancake	**5.** sailboat
7. mailbox	
8. sandbox	

Page 16

1. o, e   o, e   i, i
2. e, a   i, o   a, e
3. i, e   e, o   i, o
4. i, e   o, e
5. i, e   a, i
6. e, o   u, a

Phonics Grade 2—RBP0016

Answer Pages

Page 17

1. k(i)te, g(o)t, b(e)d, (o)pen, open

2. tr(ee), b(o)x(e)s, c(a)ke, s(ea), boxes

3. d(i)me, n(o)te, (i)ns(i)de, t(oa)d, inside

4. s(a)nd, m(ai)l, t(a)ke, p(u)ppet, puppet

5. m(i)tt(e)n, b(e)st, t(e)nt, s(o)cks, mitten

6. (e)gg, f(ee)t, r(oa)d, w(a)g(o)ns, wagons

1. open	2. boxes	3. inside
4. puppet	5. mitten	6. wagons

Page 18
1. candles	2. whistle	3. puddle
4. giggle	5. apple	6. bubbles

Page 19
2, 4, 3, 1

Page 20
nice   race   fence   rice

Page 21
Court: cones, cane, clock, case, carrot
Cecil: price, lace, cereal, pencil, ice, face, celery

Page 22
1. hard	2. soft	3. soft	4. soft
5. hard	6. soft	7. hard	8. hard
9. soft	10. soft	11. soft	12. soft

Page 23
Answer on page.

Page 24
1. backpack   2. nice, eggs, oatmeal
3. magic   4. little, huge
5. tables

Page 25
drink	branch	grass	fruit	truck
drum	price	frog	tree	

Page 26
glad: glitter, glass, globe, glue
flat: flap, flake, flame, flag
close: clock, clue, closet, class
plate: plant, play, plane, plum
black: blade, blow, blue, block
slip: slide, slipper, slow, slick

Page 27
sn	sq
sl	str
sp	sm
sc	sn
sw	st

Page 28
1. camp	2. stumps	3. tent
4. trunk	5. raft	

Page 29
body	daddy	shy
try	tiny	funny
jolly	fly	windy

Page 30

```
g y k y g i b w m i
w r j l j c y u y j
h f s f t p d h k v
y a k s d s j c y
r o c k y y a i u n
o z m p r v y y l a
s m y r y l l n u m
i r u q r o i n h m
d h b p c m l u j y
p t r y d d s b e l
```

Page 31
1. 6	2. 4	3. 8	4. 9	5. 3	6. 5

Page 32
chimp	shut	that	white
each	wish	thin	wheel
cherry	shake	teeth	when
beach	shoe	this	why

Answer Pages

Page 33
1. shop
2. chair
3. lunch
4. choose
5. what
6. peach

Page 34
1. kneel
2. know
3. knock
4. knob
5. knee
6. knit
7. knife
8. knew

Page 35
1. wreath
2. wrap
3. wrinkles
4. wrench
5. wrist
6. wren

Page 36
1. this
2. with
3. cash
4. which
5. dish
6. why
7. know
8. teeth

Page 37

Page 38
hard: card, yard, lard, shard
cart: smart, dart, part, tart
shark: dark, park, mark, lark

Page 39
1. tore
2. horse
3. porch
4. storm
5. shore
6. short

Page 40
ir: stir, third, first, shirt, chirp, skirt, firm, birth, girl
er: her, jerk, germ, clerk, after, letter, nerve
ur: burn, hurt, turtle, curve, purr, turn, fur, curl

Page 41
1. porch
2. dark
3. stormy
4. stork
5. yard
6. girl
7. shore
8. horse
9. far
10. worry
11. hurt
12. learned
13. storks
14. smart

Page 42
1. you'll
2. we'll
3. he'll
4. they'll
5. I'll
6. she'll

Page 43
1. hasn't
2. didn't
3. don't
4. haven't
5. isn't
Final question: Answers will vary but should contain the information that Justin has the chicken pox.

Page 44
1. how's   how is
2. she's   she is
3. that's   that is
4. what's   what is
5. it's   it is

Page 45
1. I have   I've
2. you have   you've
3. we have   we've
4. they have   they've

Page 46
1. let us
2. we are
3. you are
4. I am
5. they are

Page 47
1. I'm
2. you're
3. I'll
4. they'll
5. isn't
6. aren't
7. you've
8. let's
9. we're, we'll

Page 48
1. snail
2. trail
3. plain
4. day
5. stay
6. paint
7. pail
8. rain

Page 49
1. sea
2. seals
3. feet
4. meal
5. easy
6. beach

Page 50
1. toe
2. soap
3. coat
4. rainbow
5. doe
6. bowl

Page 51

Phonics Grade 2—RBP0016

Answer Pages

Page 52
moon: food, room, tooth, too, zoo, soon, boot, broom, spoon, noon

book: cook, foot, look, hook, wood, brook, took, shook, good

Page 53
1. bread 2. spread 3. weather 4. ready
5. heavy 6. feather 7. head 8. breath
Answer at bottom: a sweater

Page 54
saw, yawn, auto, laundry, hawk, fawn

Page 55
oo ea aw oo ea oo

Page 56
1. found, our, Scout, outside, town
2. know, how, loud, meow
3. Now, couch, our, house
4. Scout, brown, mouse
5. Without, sound, mouth

Page 57
ou: found, our, Scout, outside, loud, couch, house, mouse, ground, without, sound, mouth

ow: town, know, how, meow, now, brown,

Page 58
7	4
12	10
6	9

Page 59
7, 4, 6, 10, 1, 3

Page 60
crown	coil	newspaper
toy	cloud	shower
new	boy	noise

Page 61
1. wanted 2. laughed, passed
3. jumped, yelled 4. played, marched
5. cheered, raised 6. ended, rained

Page 62
e f b a c d
1. finding 2. wanting 3. cheering
4. cracking 5. sticking

Page 63
1. -ing 2. -ed 3. -ing
4. -ing 5. -ed 6. -ing

Page 64
Answers will vary.

Page 65
whale   Answers will vary.   teeth

Page 66
Answers will vary.

Page 68
ar: Marshall, hard, started, are, smart, bark, yard, arms

or: before, store, work, for

er, ir, ur: never, perfect, first, dirt, birds, turtle, turtles, water, curl, very, later, fur, purr

Page 71
1. everywhere 2. feathers, fur
3. eyes, ears, nose 4. fruit, insects
5. 600
6. caves, bridges, mines

Page 72

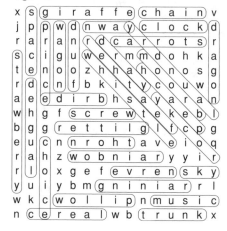

© RBP Books

Notes

Five things I'm thankful for:

1. _____
2. _____
3. _____
4. _____
5. _____

Notes

Five things I'm thankful for:

1. _____
2. _____
3. _____
4. _____
5. _____